12.40

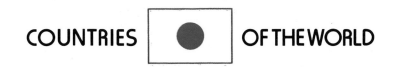

COUNTRIES OF THE WORLD

JAPAN

**Lesley Downer**

with photographs by Preben Kristensen

Illustrated by Malcolm Walker

**The Bookwright Press**
New York • 1990

*Titles in this series*

**Cover** *The Ginza, the most famous shopping street in Tokyo.*

**Opposite** *A girl at the Tanabata, or Star, Festival. The Japanese believe that on this day, the stars Vega (the Weaver Princess) and Altair (the Cowherd), who are separated lovers, cross the Milky Way and meet each other.*

© Copyright 1989 Wayland (Publishers) Ltd

First published in the United States in 1990 by
The Bookwright Press
387 Park Avenue South, New York NY 10016

First published in 1989 by
Wayland (Publishers)Ltd
61 Western Road, Hove, East Sussex, BN3 1JD,
England

**Library of Congress Cataloging-in-Publication Data**
Downer, Lesley.
  Japan/by Lesley Downer.
    p.  cm. — (Countries of the world)
  Bibliography: p.
  Includes index.
  Summary: An introduction to Japan through a survey of its geography, history, social life, religion, culture, economy, and government.
    ISBN 0-531-18306-8
    1. Japan—Juvenile literature. [1. Japan.] I. Title.
II. Series: Countries of the world (New York, N.Y.)
DS806.D69 1990
952.04'8—dc20
                  89-7374
                  CIP
                  AC
Typeset by Lizzie George, Wayland.
Printed in Italy by G. Canale and C.S.p.A., Turin.

The publishers would like to thank Japan Air Lines for its assistance with the production of this book.

# Contents

Words that appear in **bold** in the text are explained in the glossary on page 46.

# 1 Introducing Japan

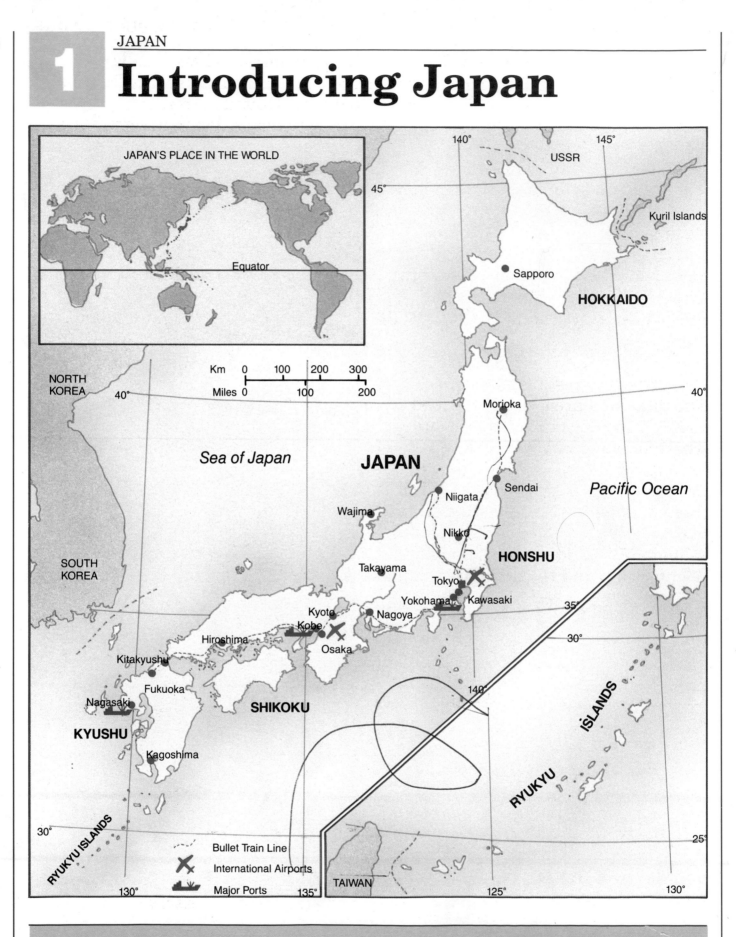

JAPAN'S PLACE IN THE WORLD

Equator

140°
145°
USSR
45°
Kuril Islands

Sapporo

HOKKAIDO

NORTH
KOREA
40°

Km 0 100 200 300
Miles 0 100 200

40°

Morioka

Sea of Japan

JAPAN

Pacific Ocean

Niigata
Sendai

Wajima

Nikko

Takayama

HONSHU

Tokyo

SOUTH
KOREA

Yokohama
Kawasaki
35°

Kyoto
Kobe
Nagoya

30°

Hiroshima

Osaka

140°

ISLANDS

Kitakyushu

Fukuoka

Nagasaki

SHIKOKU

KYUSHU

Kagoshima

RYUKYU

30°

25°

RYUKYU ISLANDS

TAIWAN

130°

135°

125°

130°

Bullet Train Line
International Airports
Major Ports

On the eastern side of the Asian continent, on the opposite side of the world from Europe, is a small island country. It is about the same size as New Zealand and has a climate similar to Great Britain's. Japan is made up of 3,922 islands, lying in an arc off of Korea, China and the eastern coast of the USSR.

Most Japanese live on the four main islands: Hokkaido in the north, the longest island, Honshu, and Shikoku and Kyushu in the south.

Japan is a very small and very crowded country. It is only about the same size as the state of Montana. The total land area is only 377,683 sq km (145,835 sq mi), and the area where people can live is even smaller, for much of the country is steep mountains. However, crowded onto these small islands is one of the world's largest populations: 125 million people, over half the population of the United States.

Today Japan is one of the world's wealthiest countries, producing industrial and household goods which are sold all over the world. If you look around your home, you will find many things that are "Made in Japan": cars, motorcycles, computers, hi-fi equipment, cameras, TV sets, even the watch on your wrist. And names like Sony, Honda and Suzuki are household words.

In the past, Japan's closest links were with its Asian neighbors, Korea and China. Nowadays it is linked more closely to the West, to those countries where it sells its goods. It also has close political ties with the United States.

But although Japan is very much part of the modern world, the Japanese are proud of their traditions. You can still see the famous Mount Fuji from Tokyo's skyscrapers, and in the spring everyone still goes to see the cherry blossoms in the **traditional** way.

*Above* The Gion Festival in Kyoto, which takes place on July 17 every year. The festival began a thousand years ago, at a time when many people in Kyoto were ill with the plague. As a way of praying to the gods to save them, they built colorful floats and drove them through the city. Today, the Gion festival is very popular and attracts huge crowds.

# 2 Land and climate

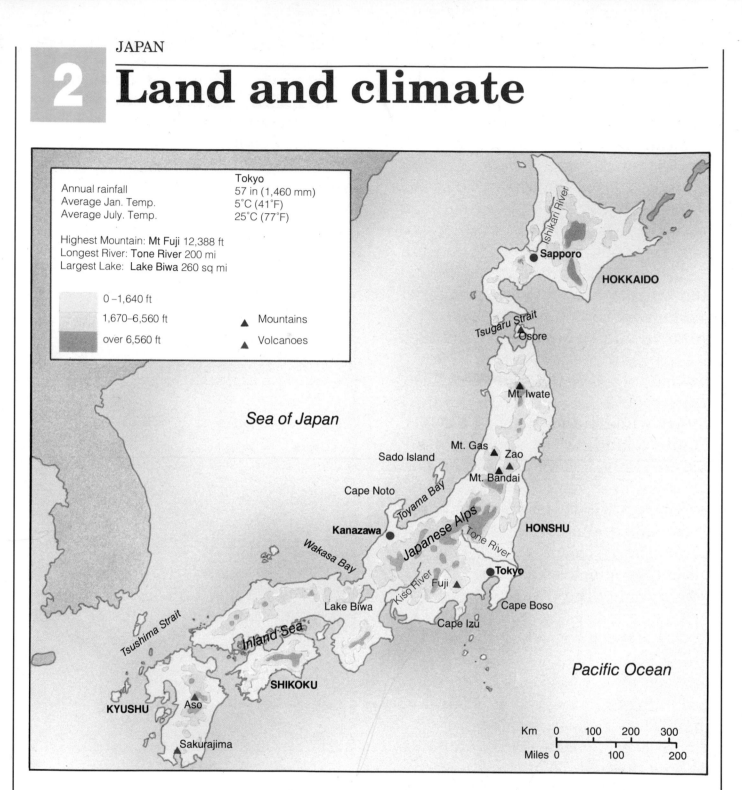

Tokyo
Annual rainfall     57 in (1,460 mm)
Average Jan. Temp.     5°C (41°F)
Average July. Temp.     25°C (77°F)

Highest Mountain: **Mt Fuji** 12,388 ft
Longest River: **Tone River** 200 mi
Largest Lake: **Lake Biwa** 260 sq mi

0 –1,640 ft
1,670–6,560 ft     ▲ Mountains
over 6,560 ft     ▲ Volcanoes

Ishikari River
Sapporo
HOKKAIDO
Tsugaru Strait
Osore
Mt. Iwate
Sea of Japan
Mt. Gas
Sado Island    ▲ Zao
Cape Noto    Mt. Bandai
Toyama Bay
Kanazawa    Japanese Alps    HONSHU
Wakasa Bay    Tone River
Kiso River    Fuji ▲    Tokyo
Lake Biwa    Cape Boso
Tsushima Strait    Cape Izu
Inland Sea    Pacific Ocean
SHIKOKU
KYUSHU    Aso
Sakurajima

Km   0    100    200    300
Miles   0      100      200

Japan is a long, narrow country. It takes seven hours on Japan's super-fast **Bullet Train** to travel from Tokyo, in the center of Honshu island, to Fukuoka, at the southernmost tip. Yet at its widest point the country is only 400 km (250 mi) across and most people live within an hour's drive of the sea. As a result, the far north and the far south of the country have very different kinds of climates and landscapes.

Most Japanese live on the island of Honshu, crowded on the plains of the east coast. To the north and west of this island are mountains, the famous Snow Country, hidden under 2-3 m (7-10 ft) of snow for five months of the year. Japan's highest mountain is beautiful Mount Fuji, a **dormant volcano** 3,776 m (12,388 ft) high.

The southern islands of Shikoku and Kyushu are **semitropical**, warm, with plenty of rain, and largely devoted to agriculture. Much of Japan's rice is grown here. Hokkaido, to the north, looks more like northern Europe. It has cold snowy winters and is covered by **pasture** land, not rice fields. This is the only part of Japan where you will see animals grazing.

Although Japan is roughly parallel to Spain and California in latitude, it has a much cooler climate, with four distinct seasons. Winter is cold, spring is wet and mild, summer is hot and humid and autumn is the **typhoon** season, with strong winds and heavy rain.

Japan is particularly prone to natural disasters. Besides the annual typhoons which often cause flooding, there are earth tremors every day and frequent earthquakes. The worst earthquake of recent years was in 1923, when most of Tokyo was destroyed. Nowadays all Japanese learn what to do in case of an earthquake, and there are regular earthquake drills in schools.

*Above* Boys on their way to school during the rainy season.

*Left* The crater of Mount Zao Volcano.

# 3 Nature and wildlife

*Above* There are many varieties of large and beautiful butterflies in Japan.

Although much of Japan is built up and industrialized, more than half is steep mountains covered with forest. This is where Japan's wildlife lives. Up in the north, wild bears roam the mountains, and there are foxes, deer, badgers and other wild animals. The island of Kyushu, in the south, is a haven for rare birds. Down on the plains, black **cormorants** dive for fish in the rivers and white herons perch beside the rice fields.

Summer is alive with insects everywhere. Different types of **cicadas** shrill from the trees and

*Below* Foxes live in the mountains and forests in the north of Japan.

*Above* A snake showing its fangs.

*Above* Bears like this Edo bear are still found in the wild in Japan.

there are dragonflies and huge bright butterflies and less pleasant insects like mosquitoes, cockroaches and hairy centipedes. Many of Japan's insects are edible. Fried grasshopper is a delicacy in the north and fried baby bees are eaten in central Japan.

In the spring people go out to the woods and riversides to collect wild plants such as burdock, horsetail shoots, fern heads and butterbur to cook and eat. In the autumn, mushroom collectors search the mountain slopes for **edible** wild mushrooms, which are sold as delicacies in the stores.

The Japanese also hunt whales for food. But whales are dying out, and under pressure from other countries, the Japanese government has agreed to phase out hunting.

The Japanese are beginning to think about the problems of their own countryside. Until 1970, the factories poured smoke into the air and chemicals into the water. The air in big cities like Tokyo became dirty and polluted. Birds and other wildlife became harder to find. Since then the government has passed a series of laws to control **pollution**. Things are improving and Tokyo's air is much cleaner, although many lakes and rivers are still heavily polluted.

# 4 JAPAN
# History

*The Sun Goddess Amaterasu. According to Japanese mythology, Amaterasu hid in a cave making the world dark until she was persuaded to come out again by the other gods.*

There are many **myths** about Japan's earliest history. Once, so the story goes, the whole world was covered with water. The god, Izanagi, and Izanami, his sister descended to earth on the "floating bridge to heaven," carrying a jeweled spear. They dipped the spear into the water and where droplets fell, the first islands of Japan appeared.

Later they had a daughter, the Sun Goddess, whose grandson was Jimmu Tenno, the first emperor. In this way, the Japanese believed, their emperor was a god who was descended from the sun.

For most of Japan's history, the capital was not Tokyo but Kyoto, the home of the emperor. A thousand years ago the princes and lords of the

Kyoto court developed a wonderful and refined culture. They spent their time composing poetry and songs and one of the court ladies wrote *The Tale of Genji*, the world's first novel.

But after this period of peace came centuries of war. The emperor no longer had any power, and the country was divided into small kingdoms which fought endlessly against each other.

Finally one ruler, Tokugawa Ieyasu, defeated all the others. In 1603 he made himself **shogun** and united the whole country under his rule. The first European traders and **missionaries** had arrived in Japan a few years before. One, an Englishman called Will Adams, was shipwrecked on the coast of Japan. He became the shogun's adviser and helped him develop a navy.

*Right* A man dressed as a samurai, or warrior, at the Jidai Matsuri festival in Kyoto.

But soon the shogun decided that the Europeans were a threat to his power. He banned all foreigners from the country and for 250 years they were not allowed to enter. Japan developed in complete isolation from the rest of the world. The shoguns continued to rule with a grip of iron, but for many Japanese this was a time of peace and prosperity.

*The Golden Pavilion at Kyoto, built as a pleasure pavilion by the Shogun Ashikaga Yoshimitsu in the fourteenth century.*

In 1853 Admiral Perry sailed into Tokyo Bay with his black ships and Japan signed a Treaty of Friendship and Trade with the United States. The young emperor Meiji took control of the country, and the Japanese, who had been cut off for so long, began to learn Western ways. They built their first telephone and railroad lines, and many Japanese scholars went abroad to study.

Japan quickly developed from a **feudal state** into a respected and feared world power. But then came

*Left* Smoke rising above the Nagasaki atomic bomb explosion and, **above**, the ruins of the city after the explosion.

World War II (1939-45). Japan invaded Manchuria, then China. They finally attacked the United States naval base at Pearl Harbor and entered the war. In 1945 the United States dropped atomic bombs on the two cities of Hiroshima and Nagasaki, forcing the Japanese to surrender. It was the first time in history that they had ever been defeated by a foreign power.

After the war, the Japanese immediately started to rebuild their country. They have been astonishingly successful; today Japan is one of the world's most important economic powers.

### Important dates

| | |
|---|---|
| 660 BC | The legendary Jimmu Tenno becomes Japan's first emperor. |
| AD 749 - 1185 | Emperor Kammu in Heiankyo Heian period: period of aristocratic culture based in Kyoto. |
| 1542 | The Portuguese (the first Europeans) reach southern Kyushu. |
| 1600 | Will Adams, an Englishman, arrives in Japan. |
| 1603-1867 | Edo Period: period of isolation. |
| 1853 | Admiral Perry sails into Tokyo Bay. |
| 1868-1912 | Meiji period: period of modernization. Edo is renamed Tokyo. |
| 1941 | Japan attacks the United States naval base at Pearl Harbor and enters World War II. |
| 1945 | Atomic bombs dropped on Hiroshima and Nagasaki. Japan surrenders. |
| 1956 | Japan joins the United Nations. |
| 1964 | With the Tokyo Olympics, Japan is accepted back into the community of nations. |

# 5 The people today

If you visit Tokyo, the most striking thing you will notice is that nearly all the people around you are Japanese. Even in the middle of this great international city, you will see very few non-Japanese faces. This is partly because Japan is an island and partly because the country was closed to foreigners for so long.

Most Japanese are smaller and lighter than Europeans, with straight black hair and olive skin. But among them are many variations. People in the north look quite different from people who come from the south.

Up in the far north, in the island of Hokkaido, lives a race called the Ainu, who are fairer and have more hair than the Japanese. Thousands of years ago, when the people who were to become the Japanese came to Japan from Korea and China and the Pacific islands, the Ainu were already there. Gradually the Japanese drove them north. Nowadays many have married Japanese and there are very few pure Ainu left.

*Below* A diagram showing how some of the characters used in Japanese writing have come from pictures.

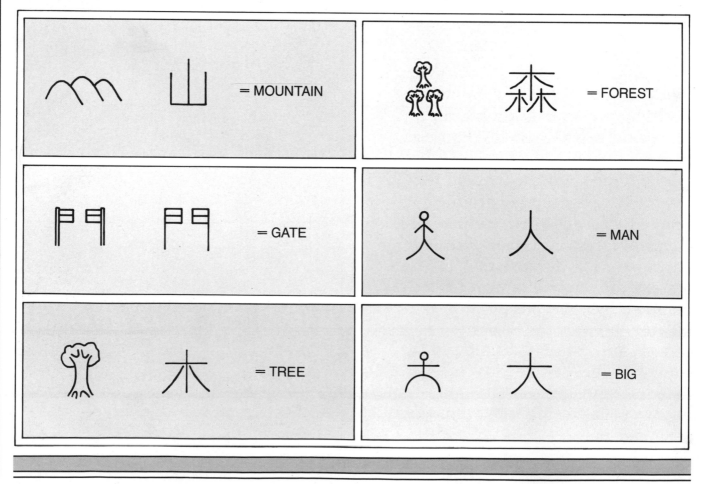

= MOUNTAIN

= FOREST

= GATE

= MAN

= TREE

= BIG

All Japanese speak the same language, Japanese. At first, Japanese writing seems very confusing. There are two kinds of alphabets and the Japanese also use many characters that are borrowed from Chinese writing. If you look carefully, you will see that many of the characters come from pictures.

*Left* Three generations of Japanese sitting on a bench in Tokyo.

*Below* Rush hour in Tokyo.

Although Japan is such a tiny country, it has the world's seventh largest population, and most of its 125 million people live in cities. As a result, it is the world's most crowded country. The city streets and railroad stations are perpetually packed with people. The population is not increasing; most families have only two children. But as people live longer, there are more and more old people. The Japanese are worried that soon they will be a society with too many old people and too few young people who are able to take care of them.

# 6 Cities

Tokyo, where 13 million people live and work, is the world's second largest city. Many of the streets are so crowded and the trains so packed that it feels like rush hour all the time! Right in the middle of Tokyo, surrounded by a park, a moat and a high stone wall, is the Imperial Palace, where the emperor lives. When the city was first built, the roads all around the palace were laid out like a maze, to make sure that the enemy could not find it. It is still easy to get lost in Tokyo.

Many parts of Tokyo are very modern, full of skyscrapers and huge department stores; but there is also an old part of the city, with street upon street of wooden houses and apartments. Most people cannot afford to live in Tokyo itself but live

*Above* A side street in the center of Tokyo.

*Left* The Ginza, Tokyo's most famous shopping street.

far away, out in the **suburbs**. It is common to spend four hours going to and from work every day.

From Tokyo, the Bullet Train whizzes south along the Pacific coast, through one city after another; first Kawasaki, then Yokohama, then Nagoya. You can travel on and on, right down to Fukuoka, 880 km (546 mi) away, and never see any countryside, only houses and factories and more houses. But you would be wrong if you thought Japan was nothing but one big city. There is plenty of beautiful countryside, but it is far from the busy Bullet Train line.

Not all Japan's cities are modern. The beautiful Kyoto is surrounded by hills. It is built next to a river and is full of ancient temples and silent gardens. Kobe, Nagasaki and Yokohama, the three towns where foreigners used to live, have streets full of Victorian houses.

**Above** Most people who work in Tokyo live in high-rise apartments on the outskirts of the city.

**Left** An old wooden house in the backstreets of Kyoto.

# 7 The family at home

**Above** *Sometimes breakfast is the only meal that all the members of one family eat together.*

Most Japanese children live with their mother, father, very often their grandparents and sometimes even their great-grandmother or great-grandfather, all together in the same house. Things are changing these days, of course, but most people still prefer to live in the traditional way. In most families it is still the father's job to go to work and earn money, while mother stays at home to look after the house and children. Gradually, however, more women are going to work, leaving grandmother to take care of the children.

While houses in the country are large and made of wood, city homes can be very small indeed. Sometimes the whole family lives in only one or two rooms. Urban land is so expensive, particularly in Tokyo, that very few people can afford to buy their home; most people live in rented apartments.

Japanese homes are very different from Western ones. Before people go in, they take off their shoes and leave them in the entrance; and while they are inside they always wear slippers or socks, never shoes. Instead of a wooden floor or a carpet, many rooms have *tatami*, thick mats made of finely woven rice straw, slightly springy under foot. Instead of inner walls there are sliding doors made of thick paper, which are taken out in the summer to make the whole house into one huge airy room.

In the room there is very little furniture, just a low table and flat cushions to sit on. Along one wall is a huge cupboard containing bedding. At night, quilts and thin mattresses which are called *futons*, are brought out and spread on the *tatami*; in the morning they are always put away again tidily.

**Above** *A Japanese family doing the weekly shopping.*

**Left** Futons, *thin mattresses are hung out over the balconies to air every morning.*

# 8 Growing up in Japan

Everyone gets up early in Japan. Children leave for school and their fathers for work around 7:30 a.m. Mothers are up before anyone else to make breakfast and pack lunches for the family. Because the streets are so safe, even little children can sometimes be seen walking to school by themselves.

Dinner time, around 6:00 p.m. is when the family sits down together – mother, children and grandparents; father does not often get home early from work. Children like Western food, such as hamburgers, french fries and ice-cream, but grandparents are used to traditional food like raw fish or seaweed. Some mothers cook and serve two different meals.

Table manners are important in Japan. Japanese children learn how to sit properly at the table, kneeling on the *tatami* matting with their legs neatly folded under them. They also learn how to use chopsticks. Young children are allowed to pick up the rice bowl and scoop rice straight into their mouths, but when they get older they have to learn how to pick up rice with chopsticks.

*Below* A boy at a baseball game.

After dinner there is homework to be done and even the smallest children have a school bag full of homework. Then there is time to play or read books and comics or to watch television. There are twelve television channels in Japan and plenty of children's programs.

Like most modern children, Japanese children love computer games, and toy shops are full of transformers and robots. But they also have dolls and other traditional toys. Little boys love baseball. In the evening they can often be seen out practicing in the street.

Then it is time for a bath – everyone has a bath every night in Japan – and finally it is time for bed.

*Above* This girl is eating her school lunch with chopsticks.

*Below* Comic books are very popular among Japanese children.

# 9 Schools and education

**Above** *Children in Japan must help clean their school every day during the lunch break.*

Children in Japan work very hard at school. At some nursery schools the children begin learning about computers at the age of three. At five, everyone begins primary school and at twelve, junior high. At fifteen they may leave school if they wish. But almost all children go on to senior high and nearly half go on to study at college.

The school day begins at 8:30 a.m. and ends at 4:30 p.m. and there is school on Saturday mornings. There are often as many as fifty pupils to a class, boys and girls mixed, and they are hardly ever tracked. Everyone wears a uniform, all the way through their school life.

Everyone has to learn to read and write, and since there are 2,000 characters as well as two alphabets to learn, it takes many years! Starting at the age of twelve everyone learns English; and they learn about the history and culture of Western countries as well as about Japan.

Japanese children have exams all the way through school. They have to work very hard to be sure of passing; if they fail, they will have to stay back a year. After a hard day at school, many children spend the evening in a *juku*, a cramming school, where they take extra classes to help them do well in their exams. Because exams are so important, most school time is spent preparing for them, learning facts by heart.

The most important exam of all is the exam to enter a university. There are 460 universities in Japan. If you get into a good one, you are certain to get a job in one of the top companies. So once you succeed in entering a university, you can relax and have fun at last! And most people do.

*Right* Children on a school trip to the zoo, eating their box lunch with chopsticks.

*Below* In small country schools, children are often given a vegetable patch to tend.

# 10 Shopping and food

The Japanese love shopping. In the center of every Japanese city are streets of arcades, roofed over to protect shoppers if it rains, lined with stores selling everything you can imagine. Often the main streets are closed to traffic. Cafés spread chairs and tables out on the street and shoppers stroll up and down.

Tokyo's most famous shopping street is the Ginza. It is full of huge glossy department stores, ten or twelve stories high, with food sold in the basement, clothes, television sets and restaurants on the upper floors. People can buy everything they need here, without ever going out. And because there is very little crime in Japan, even the most valuable goods are out on display.

Tucked in beside the big department stores there are small traditional shops. Right on the Ginza there is one store which sells only brushes and handmade writing paper; another which specializes in fans; and one that sells only combs.

Most Japanese stores are open from early in the morning until late at night. All stores stay open on Sunday and most close for a day in the middle of the week. In the cities there are

*Left* Early morning at the Tsukiji fish market in Tokyo.

*Below* Japanese stamps and currency. The unit of currency is the yen.

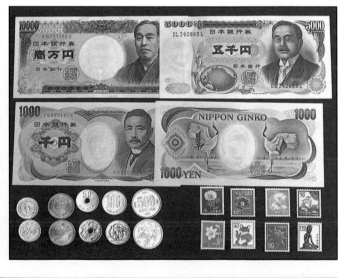

twenty-four-hour supermarkets which never close.

Most Japanese housewives shop for food every day. They may go to the basement of their local department store, where they can sample some foods before they buy them. It is always crowded and noisy, with all the food stand owners shouting "Come and buy! Come and buy!"

Markets are noisy too. The biggest and most well-known is Tsukiji, in Tokyo, where the fish and vegetables are brought in fresh every morning. For some foods, specialty shops are best. Rice shops, for example, sell only rice, in many different grades and varieties.

*Above* People buying vegetables at a morning market in a street in Kyoto.

*Below* A seed head of rice.

Rice is the most important food in Japan and the **staple** of the Japanese diet. The Japanese do not say "Let's have a meal"; they say, "Let's have some rice." Most Japanese eat rice for breakfast, lunch and dinner.

As Japan is a country of islands, and every part of it is close to the sea, there is always plenty of fish and seafood available. There are so many varieties that some have no English name. Fish is always freshly caught, so fresh that it is perfectly safe – and quite delicious – to eat raw. In fact, raw fish, *sashimi*, beautifully cut and appetizingly arranged, is one of Japan's most famous dishes.

*Below* A selection of traditional Japanese dishes.

*Above* A tea ceremony being performed at a teahouse.

Another famous dish is *sushi*, where the raw fish is pressed onto rice delicately seasoned with vinegar. It takes ten years, the Japanese say, to learn to be an expert *sushi* chef. One type of *sushi* is rolled in *nori* seaweed; in Britain *nori* is called laver and is used to make laver bread.

In the past, the Japanese did not eat meat or **dairy products** such as milk or cheese. Today, young people enjoy eating meat, although older people still eat very little. Some of the most delicious beef in the world is Japanese. There is so little spare land in Japan that cows are kept underground and fed on beer and massaged daily to make the meat tender!

Some things in Japan are very expensive; beef, for example, and other imported foods. But generally prices are much the same as they are in the United States. Some goods, like cars, television sets, refrigerators and other electrical goods are cheaper than in the West.

# 11 Sports and leisure

Sumo wrestling is Japan's national sport. Everyone loves watching two huge sumo wrestlers struggling to push each other out of the ring (which is round, not square). The *yokozuna*, the grand champions, are national heroes. Chiyonofuji, the current most successful champion, and Takamiyama, the only American to become a sumo champion, are particularly famous. The wrestlers weigh between 90 kg and 160 kg (200

*Above* Boys learning kendo, the art of the sword.

*Below* The huge Sumo wrestler, Konishiki, training for a big tournament in Nagoya.

and 350 lb) and eat enormous stews every day to build up their weight.

Many sports that are popular in the West originally came from Japan. Judo, karate, aikido and other martial arts are still very popular there. Many schoolchildren enjoy learning kendo, the art of the sword. They dress up almost like **samurai**, with a face mask, breastplate and gloves to protect them, and practice fighting with wooden swords.

*Men bathing in pools of naturally hot water at a hot spring resort.*

But the most popular sport of all is baseball. All the big cities have their own professional baseball teams and everyone supports them with enthusiasm. The most popular teams are the Yomiuri Giants, based in Tokyo, and the Hanshin Tigers, from Osaka, and the season is from April to October. In July everyone tunes in to the high school baseball games, to watch the rising young schoolboy baseball stars.

There are many quieter ways to spend leisure time in Japan. At holiday time many people go to **hot spring resorts**, to relax in pools of steaming water full of sulphur and other healing minerals. There is a big Disneyland, where Mickey Mouse greets visitors in Japanese. Of course many people spend their leisure time quietly at home, watching television, reading, or practicing a hobby such as tea ceremony or flower arrangement.

# 12 Religion

All over Japan are *torii* – gateways made of wood. They can be seen out in the fields, towering over roads, at the foot of mountains and even in the middle of a busy city, perched on an office building.

*Torii* are the entrances to Shinto shrines. According to Shinto, there are gods everywhere. Mountains, rocks, trees, rivers, are all gods; and we too become gods when we die. Until recently, the most important god of all was the emperor, who the Japanese believed was descended from the sun. But after Japan's defeat in World War II, the emperor declared that he was no longer a god, and only old people still worship him.

The job of the Shinto god is to take care of you while you are alive. When you visit a Shinto shrine, you ring the bell and clap your hands twice, to make sure that the god is awake and

**Above** *A* jizo-sama *god that takes care of the souls of children.*

**Above** *A girl visiting a Shinto shrine. The slip of paper predicts good fortune.*

*Left* A Shinto priest at the Nikko autumn festival.

listening to your prayer. Schoolchildren pray for success in exams, businessmen pray for good business, and everyone prays for health, long life and safety on the roads. Shinto priests conduct christenings and weddings and bless new cars and new offices.

Besides *torii* and Shinto shrines, there are many Buddhist temples in Japan. Most Japanese practice both Buddhism and Shinto. While the Shinto gods are believed to take care of people while they are alive, the Buddha takes care of people while they are dying and after they are dead. Buddhist priests conduct funerals. And in every traditional home there is a Buddhist shrine where the family pays respects to its ancestors.

In recent years many other religions have grown up in Japan, all of which have followers. Christianity is becoming more popular and many Japanese are now Christians.

# 13 Festivals and traditions

The Japanese have more festivals than anyone else in the world. Most important of all is the New Year Festival. On January 1, stores, offices and factories all close for three or four days and everyone goes home to their families. Outside each house is a wreath of bamboo, pine and plum branches and a rope of twisted straw to keep evil spirits away. On New Year's Eve people gather in the local Shinto shrine to warm their hands at the huge bonfire there, which burns all night long. On the stroke of midnight, huge bells ring out from all the Buddhist temples.

The third day of the third month, March 3, is Girls' Festival. Every family with girl children sets up a display of dolls, beautifully dressed in ancient court costumes and arranged on a red velvet stand.

On Children's Day, May 5, families with sons celebrate by flying huge, brightly colored paper fish, as big as kites, from their houses.

*Left* A colorful display at a New Year Market. New Year is the biggest holiday in Japan.

*Left Three generations of a Japanese family celebrating the 7–5–3 Festival.*

*Below Japanese people love huge, spectacular firework displays.*

The 7-5-3 Festival is on November 15. On this day children age seven, five and three dress up in their best **kimonos** and go to the local shrine to pray for health and long life.

Besides these festivals there are many annual events that everyone enjoys. In the spring, pink cherry blossoms flower all over the country and people go to look at them and have picnics under the trees. In autumn, the maple leaves turn brilliant shades of red, brown and gold. All summer long there are firework displays, so huge and spectacular that they always take place over water - over a river or the sea - because of the danger of fire. The fireworks are shot off from boats or from under water and explode colorfully like brilliant many-petaled flowers in the sky.

# 14 Culture and the arts

A little less than a thousand years ago, around the year 1000, a lady of the Japanese court, Murasaki Shikibu, sat down to write the adventures of a romantic young prince, Genji. What she wrote became the world's first novel, *The Tale of Genji*. Since then, many wonderful novels, poems and plays have been written, and many beautiful paintings painted. Japanese enjoy three types of theater: *Noh*, a slow dignified dance-drama in which the actors wear masks; *Bunraku*, where solemn tragedies are acted out by life-like puppets; and *Kabuki*, a colorful spectacle on a huge revolving stage, where male actors play all the parts, including women. Japan is also famous for its **woodblock prints**, by artists such as Hokusai and Hiroshige.

Besides these, there are several arts which are special to Japan. Tea ceremony is the art of making and drinking bitter green powdered tea. There is a ritual for each part of the ceremony and you have to drink the tea in exactly three and a half sips! The Japanese also study flower

*Left* A male Kabuki actor playing the part of a woman.

*Below* Flower arranging is a traditional art still popular with many Japanese people.

*Above* International pop stars like Michael Jackson have many young Japanese fans.

arranging, growing **bonsai** trees, **calligraphy**, even how to put on a kimono properly.

Japan has its own music and musical instruments: the *koto*, a stringed instrument nearly 2 m (6.5 ft) long; the *shamisen*, a kind of lute, which is often played by **geisha**; and the *shakuhachi*, a long flute made from a piece of bamboo.

Modern Japanese also enjoy Western classical music. Toru Takemitsu is a modern composer whose works are performed all over the world, and Seiji Osawa is a famous conductor.

Like young people all over the world, young Japanese have their own culture. There are many discos in every city and many popular bands and musicians. The Japanese also love Western pop singers such as Michael Jackson.

# 15 Farming and fishing

Because so much of Japan is covered by mountains, there is little very flat land left for farming — much less than in the United States or Canada. Rice is the main crop; and on every square yard of flat land there are rice fields, even squeezed in between the houses in the suburbs of cities.

Growing rice is a hard job. In the spring all the rice fields are flooded and farmers work knee-deep in water, planting the small rice shoots. Nowadays most farmers use machines to help with this job as well as with harvesting in the autumn. Weedkillers and chemical **fertilizers**

*Harvesting rice is hard work, although most farmers now have machinery to help them.*

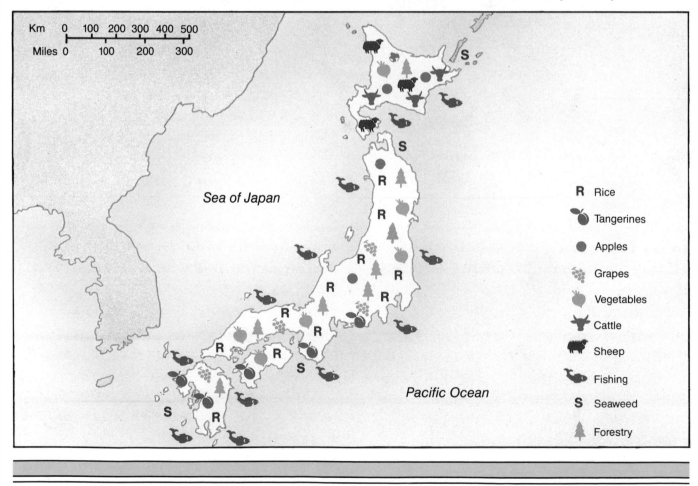

Km  0  100  200  300  400  500
Miles  0  100  200  300

*Sea of Japan*

*Pacific Ocean*

**R** Rice

Tangerines

Apples

Grapes

Vegetables

Cattle

Sheep

Fishing

**S** Seaweed

Forestry

*Right* This couple is cultivating seaweed, a popular food in Japan.

*Below* Fishing boats in the harbor at Wajima on the coast of the sea of Japan.

are also used by farmers to increase the size of the crop.

In the past everyone ate rice at every meal. But now tastes are changing. People are eating less rice and more Western foods like bread, meat and milk. As a result, there is more rice than can be sold, and this causes the price to drop. The government has to boost farmers' incomes by giving them **subsidies** and is encouraging them to switch to other crops.

Melons, mandarin oranges, grapes and other fruit and vegetables are also important crops in Japan. Most Japanese farms are very small, and there is little room to keep animals.

As Japan is a country of islands, the sea is very important. Japanese fishing fleets trawl the ocean for tuna, cod, sardines and other fish while smaller boats fish off the coast for mackerel and shrimps.

There are many fish farms. Saltwater fish like yellowtail tuna and sea bream are kept in sheltered bays, and there are large freshwater ponds for breeding eel, carp and rainbow trout.

The Japanese also cultivate seaweed for food. Laver seaweed *(nori)* is grown in Kyushu and kelp *(kombu)* is gathered around the coast of Hokkaido.

# 16 Industry

Many of the things you use every day are probably made in Japan. Our homes and offices are full of Japanese goods, from toys, electronic games, transformers, personal stereos, calculators, cameras and watches, to television sets, video recorders, compact disc players and cars. People buy Japanese goods because they are cheap, reliable and top quality, and the Japanese are perpetually coming up with new and more advanced products.

Japan is one of the world's most important industrial nations. It has made much of its wealth through manufacturing and exporting goods to other countries.

In the sixties and seventies, its most important products were steel, ships, cars, television sets, video recorders and cameras. Today the steel and shipbuilding industries are in difficulty, partly because of competition from new companies in South Korea.

In the eighties, Japanese companies are concentrating on high-technology products such as

**Below** *Inside the Nissan car factory in Kanagawa. Much of the work is now done by robots, not people.*

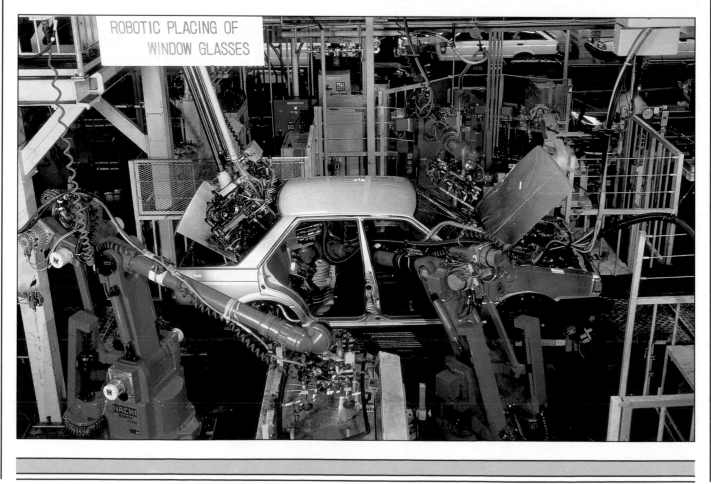

ROBOTIC PLACING OF WINDOW GLASSES

**Main Exports:**
Machinery, Cars, Metals,
Textiles

**Main Imports:**
Coal and Oil, Metal Ore, Raw
Materials, Foodstuffs

*Left* Japanese industry
produces all the latest models
of electronic and TV
equipment.

*Below* Not all Japanese
people work in factories.
Iseburo Kado, a famous
lacquerware artist, still works
in the traditional way at his
studio in Wajima.

semi-conductors and computers and
developing robots to be used in
industry. They are also working on
many exciting developments for the
future: high definition television,
computers with artificial intelligence,
and robots that can take over routine
manufacturing jobs so that human
beings are free to do more creative
ones.

There are many reasons for the
success of Japanese industry. One is
that a Japanese company is rather
like a big family. Once you have
joined, you never leave. You are
guaranteed a job for life. The
company provides a home and a
share in the profits, a school for your
own children, sometimes a hotel for
your vacation. As a result, Japanese
employees work as hard as they can
for their firm and rarely go on strike.

# 17 Transportation

The Bullet Train, the *Shinkansen*, is Japan's most famous train, and a symbol of the country. It has a nose like a bullet and travels at a maximum speed of 250 kph (155 mph) along a track specially built for it. For many years it was the fastest train in the world. Now some European trains are faster. But the Japanese are working on a hover-train which will glide above an electric rail at twice the speed of the Bullet.

**Below** *The Japanese* Shinkansen, *or Bullet Train, is one of the fastest and most punctual trains in the world.*

**Above** *A Japan Air Lines jet. In the background is snow-covered Mt. Fuji, the highest mountain in Japan.*

The Bullet Train is still, like all Japanese transportation systems, the most punctual in the world. If it is more than a few minutes late, half your fare will be returned to you! In 1987 the Japanese opened the longest railroad tunnel in the world, from Honshu to the island of Hokkaido; and soon it will be possible to travel between all of Japan's four main islands by train.

Japanese trains are very crowded. At rush hour, in some Tokyo stations, there are even white-gloved staff pushing people into suburban trains to help the doors close!

The roads too, in Japan, are crowded, as more and more people own cars. Until 1970, the air in Tokyo was very polluted from the fumes of all the traffic. Then the government passed a law setting a limit to the amount of poisonous fumes, such as carbon monoxide, which cars could give off. Now all Japanese cars are built to this standard, and the air is much cleaner.

Distances are great in Japan. It takes ten hours to travel from one end of the Bullet Train line to the other; yet this takes you across only half the country.

Many people prefer to fly. There are airports in all the big cities and frequent and regular flights by Japan Air Lines and other airlines. On some planes, as you take off, you can watch a video of what the pilot sees and feel as if you are sitting beside him in the cockpit.

**Above** Hundreds of bicycles parked outside a station on the outskirts of Tokyo.

**Below** Traffic in Tokyo is monitored by computer at a central control office.

# 18 Government

Japan has a parliamentary system. There are elections every three to four years, when everyone over twenty can vote. Parliament is known as the Diet. It consists of two houses: the House of Representatives, with 512 members, and the House of Councillors. But, although voters in Japan have several different parties to choose from, the Liberal Democratic Party has actually held power for more than thirty years. Its leader

*Right* The Japanese government. Since 1947, the emperor has had no political power.

*Below* The Japanese Diet, or Parliament.

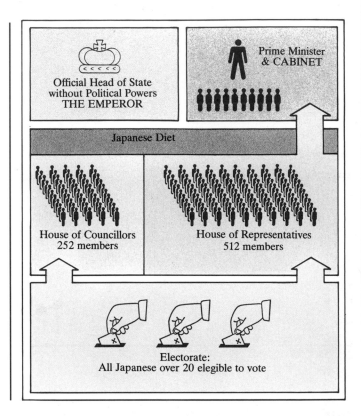

Official Head of State without Political Powers
THE EMPEROR

Prime Minister & CABINET

Japanese Diet

House of Councillors
252 members

House of Representatives
512 members

Electorate:
All Japanese over 20 elegible to vote

*Right* A local policeman standing outside his police box in a suburb of Tokyo.

*Below* The Japanese are so law abiding that sometimes only plastic policemen are needed to remind them of regulations.

is Noboru Takeshita, who became Prime Minister in 1987.

In the past the emperor too had power. But in 1947, after World War II, it was declared that he would be a symbol of the state, like Britain's queen.

At the same time, the Japanese drew up a "Peace Constitution," saying that they would never attack another country and would only take part in a war if it were absolutely necessary, to defend their country. In 1967 they adopted three nonnuclear principles: never to produce nuclear weapons, never to possess them, and never to allow any into Japan. As a result, the Japanese army, navy and airforce are very small. But there are large numbers of United States troops stationed all over Japan.

Japan has an unusually low crime rate. There is very little mugging or murder. When crimes are committed, the police usually succeed in finding and arresting the criminal. As a result, even big cities are safe. One reason for this is the large police force. There is one police officer for every thirty houses, and policeman always know everyone on their beat and often drop in to visit them. Much of the crime in Japan is organized by the *yakuza*, gangs that operate rather like the Mafia in the United States.

# 19 Facing the future

*Left* Miss Takako Doi, chairperson of the Socialist Party, is one of the many women who are beginning to hold powerful positions in Japanese society.

*Below* An old woman from a country rice-growing farm.

Japan is racing into the future faster than any other country in the world. A hundred years ago, when Europe was in the middle of the **Industrial Revolution**, Japan was still a **medieval** country of samurai, peasants and storekeepers, completely cut off from the rest of the world.

Today it has caught up with the West and overtaken it. It is probably the most technologically advanced country in the world. The economy is booming, most people are well off, and the country is playing a more important part in world affairs. Every year, more Japanese travel abroad, on business and on vacation, and every year there are more foreign faces on the streets of Tokyo.

Even in the last ten years Japan has changed enormously. These changes cause problems as well as bringing benefits. Young people growing up today are used to Western ways; they wear Western clothes and eat Western food. Older people are afraid that the traditional culture and way of life will be lost.

In the past, when young people married they always lived with their parents in the same house.

Nowadays, many prefer to live on their own; so when their parents grow old, there is no one to look after them. The Japanese are a healthy race and old people live for a very long time. Soon there will be more old people who are retired than there are young ones who can work and support them. This is another problem for Japan.

In the last few years the Japanese have become more and more concerned about their environment. Because there are so many factories, much of the countryside has been spoiled. In many big cities the air is very dirty, even though there are now laws against pollution.

But basically the future looks rosy for Japan. The Japanese are a hard-working and resourceful people and will certainly find solutions to their problems.

**Above** Businessmen in Tokyo's modern commercial district.

**Left** The torii gate entrance to a Shinto shrine. Although Japan is one of the world's richest and most modern countries, Japanese people still value their traditional way of life.

# Glossary

**Bonsai** The art of keeping trees and shrubs very small by cutting their roots and branches.

**Bullet Train** One of the fastest trains in the world. It travels at 250 km per hour (155 mph) along the Pacific coast of Japan.

**Calligraphy** The art of handwriting.

**Cicada** An insect somewhat like a grasshopper, found in tropical countries in summertime. It makes a noise by vibrating a membrane in its thorax.

**Cormorant** A large black bird that lives on rivers or by the coast and dives for fish.

**Dairy products** Food products produced in a dairy: milk, butter, cheese and cream.

**Dormant volcano** A volcano that is live but is not active at present.

**Edible** Anything which is safe to eat.

**Fertilizers** Chemicals or natural substances added to soil or sprayed on growing plants to make them bigger.

**Feudal state** A medieval country where farmers are protected by a lord or baron; in return for their protection, the farmers must pay taxes to their lord and serve in his or her armies.

**Geisha** A Japanese woman trained in the arts of singing and dancing.

**Hot spring resort** Place where naturally hot water, full of minerals (considered as healing), gushes out of the ground. People go there to bathe.

**Industrial Revolution** The period of history, from the late eighteenth century onward, when Europe was developing machinery and factories.

**Kimono** The traditional Japanese costume: a loose robe with wide sleeves. People still wear kimonos when they dress up for special occasions.

**Medieval** Having to do with the Middle Ages in Europe (approximately between AD 1000 and 1500), when modern industries had not yet been developed.

**Missionary** Someone sent out, often abroad, on religious work.

**Myth** An ancient story about gods, heroes and supernatural happenings that may try to explain natural events like the weather, sunrise and sunset and so on.

**Pasture** Fields where animals graze.

**Pollution** Dangerously high levels of dirt and poisonous substances in the air or in water; usually produced by factories or car exhausts.

**Samurai** A Japanese warrior.

**Semitropical** A country which has hot, or tropical, weather for part of the year.

**Shogun** The title of rulers of Japan before 1868.

**Staple** The most important food in one's diet.

**Subsidy** Money given by the government to farmers or industries in need of assistance.

**Suburb** A district where people live, on the outskirts of a city.

**Traditional** The opposite of modern; doing things the old way.

**Typhoon** Strong winds and driving rain. The typhoon season in Japan is September.

**Woodblock prints** Pictures carved on wooden blocks, then printed.

# Books to read

Downer, Lesley. *Japanese Food and Drink* (Bookwright, 1988).

Jacobsen, A.P. and P. Kristensen. *A Family in Japan* (Bookwright, 1985).

Kawamata, Kazuhide. *We Live in Japan* (Bookwright, 1984).

Lye, Keith. *Asia and Australasia* (Gloucester, 1987).

Pilbeam, Mavis. *Japan* (Franklin Watts, 1988).

Samarasekara, Dhantala. *I am a Buddhist* (Franklin Watts, 1987).

Snelling, John. *Buddhism* (Bookwright, 1986).

Tames, Richard. *Passport to Japan* (Franklin Watts, 1988).

# Picture acknowledgments

All photographs were taken by Preben Kristensen with the exception of the following: Chapel Studios 3, 5, 7 (bottom), 8 (top), 11, 12, 17 (bottom), 31, 32, 33 (both), 45 (bottom); Michael Holford 10; Japan Air Lines 40 (top); Japan National Tourist Organization 26; Orion Photographic 29, 47; Oxford Scientific Films 8 (bottom), 9 (both); Tony Stone (cover); Wayland Picture Library 13 (both), 34 (left), 42.

The publishers would also like to thank Nikko Hotels for their help with the photograph on page 27.

# The Chick
# and the Duckling

Translated from the Russian of V. Suteyev

## by Mirra Ginsburg
## Pictures by Jose & Ariane Aruego

Macmillan Publishing Co., Inc.
New York

Collier-Macmillan Publishers
London

Macmillan Publishing Co., Inc.
866 Third Avenue, New York, N.Y. 10022
Collier-Macmillan Canada Ltd.
Toronto, Ontario

Library of Congress catalog card number: 74-188773

Printed in the United States of America

10  9  8  7  6  5  4  3  2

The text was translated from the Russian
*Tsyplenok i Utenok* (The Chick and the
Duckling) of V. Suteyev.

The four-color illustrations were prepared as
pen-and-ink line drawings with halftone overlays.
The typeface is Avant Garde Book.

to Libby

A Duckling came out
of the shell.

"I am out!" he said.

"Me too," said the Chick.

"I am taking a walk,"
said the Duckling.

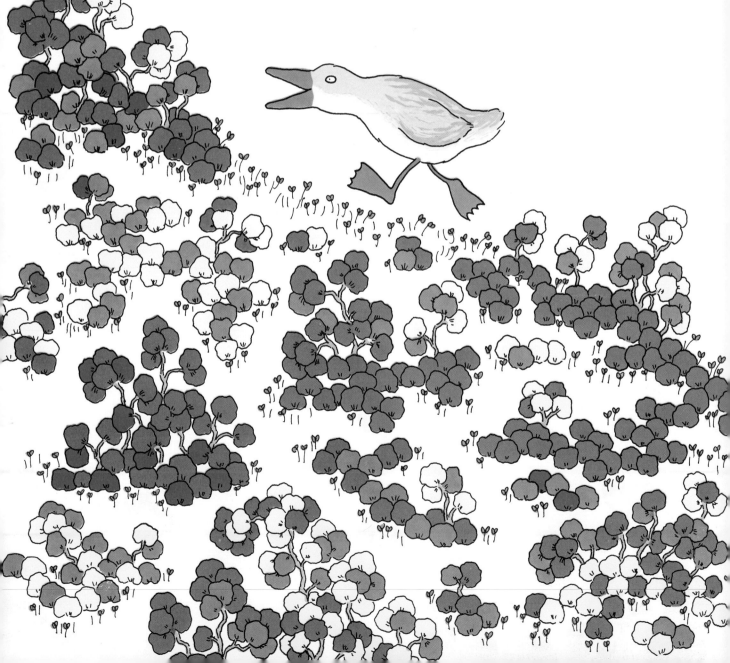

"Me too,"
said the Chick.

"I am digging a hole,"
said the Duckling.

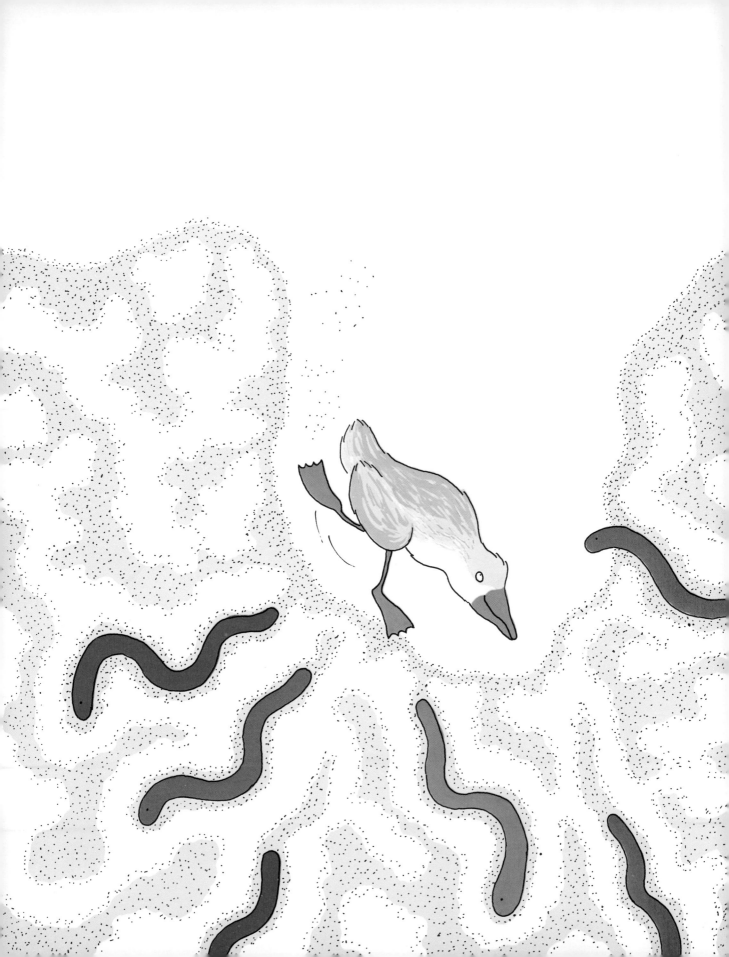

"Me too,"
said the Chick.

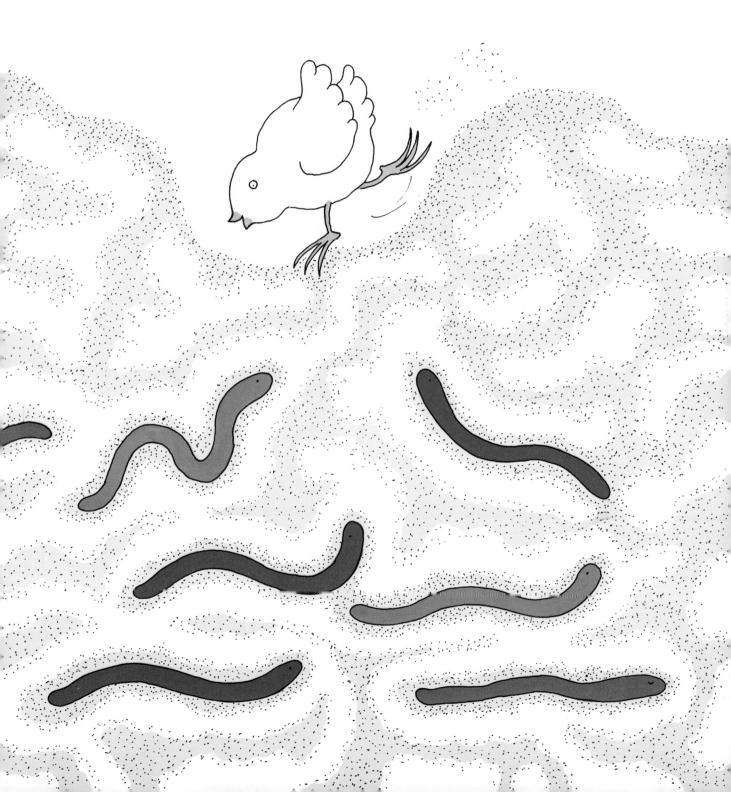

"I found a worm,"
said the Duckling.

"Me too,"
said the Chick.

"I caught
a butterfly,"
said the
Duckling.

"Me too,"
said the Chick.

"I am going for a swim,"
said the Duckling.

"Me too,"
said the Chick.

# "I am swimming,"
said the Duckling.

"Me too!"
cried the Chick.

# The Duckling pulled
# the Chick out.

"I'm going for another swim,"
said the Duckling.

"Not me,"
said the Chick.